SPARKLING SANDS

SRIZEN KHANEJA

Copyright © Srizen Khaneja
All Rights Reserved.

This book has been published with all efforts taken to make the material error-free after the consent of the author. However, the author and the publisher do not assume and hereby disclaim any liability to any party for any loss, damage, or disruption caused by errors or omissions, whether such errors or omissions result from negligence, accident, or any other cause.

While every effort has been made to avoid any mistake or omission, this publication is being sold on the condition and understanding that neither the author nor the publishers or printers would be liable in any manner to any person by reason of any mistake or omission in this publication or for any action taken or omitted to be taken or advice rendered or accepted on the basis of this work. For any defect in printing or binding the publishers will be liable only to replace the defective copy by another copy of this work then available.

THE CO-AUTHORS

Contents

Contents

Contents

Foreword

This anthology is a work of fiction. The compiler has tried her best to edit and assemble the content of the co-authors and make it plagiarism free. In case of any plagiarism detected, the compiler is not responsible, Co-authors will be solely responsible for their own content.

Acknowledgements

It's hard to fulfill a promise to deliever something immaculately detailed but the Co-Authors of this book has done that. I am greatly thankful for tha patience my Co-Authors have shown that has made this book possible. This book is solely dedicated to these people who made it possible and thier beautiful work that is showcased here

Love

Srizen Khaneja

CHAPTER ONE

Srizen Khaneja

<u>IT'S JUST A LITTLE HARD!</u>
One random day,
in one random way,
Can I call you?
Can I call you and tell you,
how I feel?
Can I call you and tell you,
I feel hollow inside?
It's not a good feeling.
I feel lost and think, who I am asking these questions
to?
I don't have anyone,
I don't know anyone who I feel comfortable with.
I feel like I don't trust anyone anymore.
I can not rely on anyone anymore.
Why do we feel this way?
Why do we feel that happiness is to be shared and
sadness is to be kept inside?
Why these feelings are brushed aside?
I sit alone and think who can I talk to?
Is there anyone who I trust enough to talk about my
feelings ?

Is there anyone who wouldn't use them against me in some manner?
Is there anyone who won't have a negative opinion on them?
Is there anyone who'll not expect this human being who isn't ideal or perfect?
I find no one.
I feel like humanity is the lost cause.
Love is the lost cause.
Acceptance is not so acceptable.
All they expect you to be is not messed up and stable.
Why wouldn't they understand that truth isn't what you expect?
Perfection is unattainable and smiles aren't always natural.
Why does everyone have to classify everything right or wrong why can't something be neutral?
Why are only actions taken into consideration and intentions are ignored?
Why is it important to fit into a box?
Why can't unconventionality be one of our society's building blocks?
Why can't we be comfortable with being made uncomfortable by someone's life choices?
P. S. :- it's easy to judge but hard to go through the judgement, it's important to be kind enough to realize that the people who we give our personal negative judgements about are also humans.

CHAPTER TWO

Noor Tabassum

<u>Most Awaited Desire</u>

I still remember my darling, That mysterious and velvety evening, When my curious eyes saw you smiling, You were cladded in yellow and blue, Imparting peculiar waves which kept me glued, That mischievous smile of yours, That captivating fragrance emitted by you, Drew me into an unknown gravity towards you, And I was lost in your vicinity. I flew in the air around you, I could not control my emotions nor my eyes, I do not know how I rooted up towards you, Neither did you commit nor deny, Leaving me to burn in a weird smokeless fire, I kept anticipating a sign from you, But you were lost in your world of desire, I still wait for you my darling, I still crave that one mesmerizing touch from you.

............NOOR...............

CHAPTER THREE

Nandini Sood

<u>'Pjs' a perfect metaphor for love</u>
Beauty,looks and price,
Very different words but not so different.
Beauty is judged by looks and looks come for a price.
In life you always have to pay a 'P',
Price or peace,
Who decided that you need to look beautiful to be loved
.

This all is fed in our subconscious mind knowingly or unknowingly.
We do that because we have trained our minds to think that way,
And our subconscious doesn't have a logic to argue with us,that's why it happens.
Everyone says not to judge a book by its cover but deep down this is what everybody does.
People don't need to have those fillers to attract love in their life;
These things fade away with time.
If you want to find real love;
Look for something that fills your soul,
Brings peace,
Helps you get a good night's sleep.

"Love needs to be like your pjs"
Helps you to relax and let your body breathe.
It being the first thing you want to reach after a long day.
     Though it should not be like a drug;
That gives a temporary high and flushes you from inside.
     A perfect pj may be hard to find but will be worth it.
Just keep feeding your conscience with all the positive energy.
It will help you find that perfect pj!
     - Nandini Sood

CHAPTER FOUR

Gourav Nayak

Yes, this story is incomplete but it is a whole on it's own. It was not only 7 months,5 days that we spent together, it was the entire time we have got to love each other and we never missed a single chance to wrap each other in our imaginary arms. Different states but distance never separated us. We had millions of dreams with a hope we wanted to make them true. Whenever I talked to her it seemed like we were sitting together holding each other's hands. We spent many hours on phone calls but felt like we talked only for some minutes. Our closeness was too faster for calendar or clock and we had crossed all the levels of closeness in just 3-4 months. Yes, it was possible because we spent our summer and monsoon nights together chatting. She was the only one I wanted to make mine. Then we faced a very Terrible thing that I never ever thought about called "Religion". We tried a lot to save everything but situations went wrong. We remained incomplete

CHAPTER FIVE

Yuvraj Singh

1.कुछ इस तरह मेरे दिल से उतर रही है वो.. ! जिस शख़्स से नफ़रत थी मुझे उस शख़्स के साथ दिख रही है वो...!!

2.बहुत दिनों बाद मेरे सपनों में वो आना शुरू कि है..! लगता है अपने नये वाले के साथ लडना शुरू की है...!

3.मुझे छोड़ के किसी और के साथ दिल लगा रही है, और मेरा दिल तोड़ के वो हस्ते हुए जा रही है, और मै भी कितना पागल हू उससे आखिरी दफ़ा बात किया था तो यही बोल आया कि तू हस्ती रह अच्छी लगती है, मुझे लगता है कि वो इसी बात की सजा मुझे दे रही है

4.दिल से दिल मिल जाये तो सजा देते है ये लोग.. प्यार के एहसासो को डूबा देते है लोग.. और अगर कही गलती से एक इंसान की आदत पड़ जाए तो तड़पा देते है लोग.. और तुम इंसानो कि बात करते हो.. अरे इंसानो को साथ देखना तो छोडो़... यहाँ परिंदा भी साथ बैठ जाए तो उडा़ देते है लोग..

5. काश अगर होती गिरफ़्तारी तेरी नजरो मे, तो हम दिल को उम्र कैद की सजा दिलवा देते।

Karmanya Pahwa

I wonder if I will ever get myself back, Lost in those
waves
Sometimes a couch potato, On the other half's I crave
for my Romeo ,
Is it fine for a tender age ? Who is leaving the study
cage !
Distractions coming my way, Chapters like refraction
are pending From last two sundays !
From ages I am trying to work on one lesson .
Interestingly, books are on the shelf with a single line ,
Which is not underlined!
Then he asks me to help yourself, And I wonder when
will I get myself?

CHAPTER SEVEN

Sanjeev Maurya

An Ode To Death
>He came riding the black buffalo,
>Penetrating the virgin night,
>To show the start to the end,
>A sling to your neck-
>Of his lasso; you scream.
>Beg and fight,
>With all your might,
>But the feeble body gave up
>- Gave up at the very start,
>At the very sight.
>Now the soul is tied,
>Dragged along the milky way,
>To the other side of the river,
>To be judged and weighed-
>Weighed for your sins and evil.
>No running now,
>Will have to pay for what is sowed,
>Grown and reaped,
>Of and on the earthen,
>For the five elements.

CHAPTER EIGHT

AJ Potter

वो रात भी कोई शब-ए-क़यामत ही रही होगी,
जब उस ज़ालिम मुस्कुराहट पे क़ुर्बान हो गए।।
कभी कहे थे यूँ ही कुछ अल्फ़ाज़ उसने होंठों से,
और उम्र भर के लिए वो हमको कलाम हो गए।।
कटते रहे ताउम्र उसकी नज़रों की धार से मगर,
उसकी हिफ़ाजत को उसकी नियाम हो गए।।
ले लेकर उसका नाम महफ़िल में हर वक़्त,
हम अपनी महफ़िल में ही गुमनाम हो गए।।
कर दी रोशनी सारी हमने हिस्से में उसके,
हम अपने हिस्से में अन्धेरी शाम हो गए।।
मिटि गयी हर ख़्वाहिश तेरे इश्क़ में ऐ आलिम,
अब तेरे बोल ही मेरे लिए अहकाम हो गए।।
वजूद कुछ ना बाकी बचा अब अपना ख़ुद का,
वो हमारे ना हुए मगर हम उसके नाम हो गए।।
रहा इश्क़ बाकी ना अब तुझमें ना मुझमें,
तेरे मेरे इश्क़ के ये कैसे अंजाम हो गए।।
पुकारा तूने था कभी किसी सावन में ऐ 'भूमि,'
बारिश बन कर गिरि, तेरे होंठों के जाम हो गए।।

CHAPTER NINE

Mohanapriy.K

Farming

What a joy it is to sow a seed in the soil and watch it grow!

That too would be so beautiful to see that little plant visible above the soil sprouting from the seed.

How special are the flowers that bloom from the plant that we germinate from seed.

There are no words to describe it!

When you look at it like that the farmers that we all eat and produce are so high.

They are the ones we should worship in keeping with God.

But are we doing that?

But we have to do just that.

Our government must take a lot of effort and action for this.

We should all have sown the seeds for a lot of trees and plants in life.

We should also make this our fasion and favorite hobby.

CHAPTER TEN

Anjali Jain

Far apart from the human vision,
    There's a deep flowing sea,
    No, no this is not an ordinary sea
    It's very special my dear,
    The 'Red Moana'
    As soon as we hear RED
    There is plethora of stress,
    Bubble of worries,
    Floating in our veins,
    Like octopus has fastened our blain
    Only specific gender can dive into it.
    As if we are meant to do this
    We are only lifeguard,
    & we are only drowning,
    Confused what's going?
    We call this by varied names
    'Special Day', 'Birthday', 'Aunt Day',
    Gosh, You can't imagine,
    It's far from your itsy-bitsy heads,
    Because it's the "Periods"
    The silent bane ruling our body,
    The odd behaviour commanding our routine,
    The society norms increasing our difficulties,

The damn thinking troubling us more than anything,
In great dilemma what to do & whatnot.
It comes with tension,
Goes with confusion,
Making us think why it's so important
Pain has its own reason,
& Sufferer has it's own motive.
At the end we are survivors
Overcoming the obstacles,
Defeating the problems,
Winning our battles,
Soon will break the untouchable wall.

CHAPTER ELEVEN

Pranjal Patil

earing through my heart,
Never found you in part;
Still longed for your depart,
Like I am a little hard....
Crashed you up with thunder,
My heart that is on burner;
Never stalk like a fighter,
Or I will come a little harder....
Thought like I was naive,
Dumped you in a cave;
Thriftily over the scorching wave,
No way, I am A Nicked Grave...

Agam Sachdeva

MY MAN (DAD)

You May have thought I didn't see,

Or that I didn't hear Life lessons that you taught me,

But I got every word.

You'd thought that I missed it all,

lost And now when we grew apart And I forgot my favourite ball!?

But, dear dad I picked every lesson And applied it somewhere.

It's still written in my heart with the darkest of ink.

Umm, without you I wouldn't be anything

I won't even be a good being

And also no manners,

if you weren't there To teach me all of it And something, on Netflix also bing.

I am all grown up

Yes, your little Baby is now grown up

But, I haven't forgotten all the value you taught me

And only because of you, I am always in glee.

To be honest,

I wouldn't match your level tven if I go on knee.

You are that special, You are that important, That is honey to bee.

Dear daddy, You be always with me
And lastly I Love you, papa.
The One behind all the life's glee.

Zainab Saboowala

<u>ज़िन्दगीकासफर</u>
धुंधली सी थी मंजिल
सपनो का पता ना था
अनजाने से राहों में
अपनों का पता ना था
बातें थीं अनकही
लफ्जों का पता ना था
ज़िन्दगी के इस सफर में
मुझे मुझी का पता ना था।

Krishna Motwani

All of the words are for the feelings of girls heart,
She too takes time to forgot all dark phases and again to start.
She was born with fear,
She is also a human, don't let her heart to tear.
She fears to go out of the home,
All the time she fears to come.
She too have her dreams,
Don't do such things, her heart too screams.
She hesitates to talk to anyone,
Only a girl can understand this pain otherwise no one.
Although a girl's life is too tough,
She is bold that's enough.
Let her soul to live her freely,
Let her too live merrily!

CHAPTER FIFTEEN

Sakshi Sharma

दोस्ती भी अजीब सा नशा है,

दोस्त मिल जाते अगर अच्छे,

लगते हैं हर पल सच्चे,

वो हर दिन मुझे याद है,

जो गुज़ारा मैंने तुम सबके साथ है,

हँसते थे साथ में, तो रोये भी तो थे,

खाते थे साथ में, और सोते भी तो थे,

याद है मुझे हर वो पल,

किया हॉस्टल में हर पागलपन,

आँखों की वो नमी भी याद है,

जब हुये विदा हम घर को,

रोये ऐसे जैसे बिछड़ गया जहाँ हो,

हर मस्ती वो याद है, मेस का चुराया खाना,

और आधी रात की मैगी का स्वाद आज भी लाजवाब है,

हॉस्टल में बम, और वार्डन को तंग,

किये हुए सब लम्हें मुझे याद है,

असाइनमेंट और पीरियोडिकिल्स की वो काली रात,

हो ट्यूसडे का खाना या मंडे की रात,

हो सर्दी की एपी फ़ज़िज़ या रात की कॉफ़ी का नशा,

सब कुछ बड़ा ही यादगार है,

सुबह की ठण्ड में डरावनी आवाज़ें,
और रात के अँधेरे में भूतिया बातें,
बाथरूम में स्पीकर्स, और नहाने की लाइन,
कितना सब तो था, जो आज भी वैसे ही याद है,
वो दिन वापस आ जायें फिर से,
बस यही करती हूँ दुआ,
यारियां किस्मत से मिलती हैं यारो,
मिले सबको ऐसे यार, जिनकी यादें दें रुला,
दोस्ती भी अजीब सा नशा है,
दोस्त मिल जाए अगर अच्छा,
लगता है हर पल सच्चा ,
दोस्ती भी अजीब सा नशा है|

CHAPTER SIXTEEN

Harkirat Singh aka Harry

God's Bath
   Standing Alone
Having Random Thoughts in my mind
Waiting for Someone
To talk for a while
   It's been a Week
Since my last face to Face Conversation
My Brain is somewhere else and
My heart is desperate
   Want to relive my Past, again
But it's not possible
As this is how life Behaves.
   Was Excited to shift to the new City
Away from family and duties
Wasn't aware
How life would be so Pity
   Missed my mother
Never this much
Want to sleep in her lap
As nights are not smoother

Want to cry for some minutes
To Pour out my pain
But eyes are taking Hours
To make a fine way
Suddenly, A drop of rain
Fall over my face
Hugging me tight
To express my pain
The rain started falling hard
I close my eyes,
To enjoy a god's bath
It Seemed that divine Power is healing me
As I cried after a long time
God's bath insisted me to express myself
To enjoy this Short Life

Parvadha Samuvel

<u>A DECEPTIVE LOVE</u>
I loved you deeply - but
Am I a passby for you?
I believed you are my world strongly-but
Am not even worth as grass for you?
I expected all love from you truely- but
Am I a begger for you?
I gifted you whatever you need happily-but
Am I a machine for you?
I understood everything about you finally-but
Am still trying to unlove you!
I realised my mistake painfully-but
Am not able to convince me about losing you!

CHAPTER EIGHTEEN

Shubhamay Biswas

In my lonely moments,
I weave dreams of you,
& my heart answers me every time,
How much I am in love with you,
Every problem solves automatically,
When you are in my eyes, &
Gives me new excuses,
Gives a measure of seasons,
Gives me rain of dreams in my eyes,
Gives me intentions,
Gives me promises,
Gives me shelter in your heart...

CHAPTER NINETEEN

Sowndharya

<u>The tiny little spark</u>
In this sparkling world
I am a little spark
That is shining outside
With so many dark
Memories inside
I put a smile as a cover
To my sorrow but, why
I hide my sorrow to
Make myself so strong
As time pass by when
I become the brightest
Sparkle of the world
My darkest side
Remind me of how
Hardworking I was
And I am. So, let's rock
The world with our talent.

Shiny Jaiswal

She was meek and shy,
A little of everything nice,
She hardly ever spoke,
But had lot to say,
A voice in her head screamed loud,
Urged her to confront her doubts,
But she was afraid of rejection,
So she stayed silent while they all chatted,
She wasn't pretty,
Nor what you would call easy on eyes,
She was just odd looking girl,
With lot on her mind,
She blended well in background,
People often looked past her,
One day a boy looked right in her eyes,
Saw a soul more beautiful than skin,
Fell for her in one sweep,
That was all she needed,
A soul to love her for who she was,
And just like that she blossomed,
Into a girl of words and wisdom.

CHAPTER TWENTY-ONE

Onadipe Habeeb

A sub-abode below my home
  With different sand of the earth
  Sandy, loamy and clay
  All sparkling like that of the radiant sun
  That shares light across the globe.
  With utmost sincerity
  Always peeping like that
  Of a baby, the sand, running for an angry mother
  To know whether or not she has ease chase.
  Mama and Papa both blind
  Inferior in almost all ramifications
  To know the aim of our visitors
  With gifts and phlegmatic to.
  My tomorrow lies in the sand
  It's there my territory would originates
  Now losing my own tomorrow inheritance to a
sojourner
  Just for my parents blindness.
  Hospitality is our pride
  In the land my home stands
  We feed them, dress them
  But they pay us handsomely.
  A pause the family said?

Foundation of our home shaking
Digger pounding on the home below my home
Only to find out
Brightest of its colour scanty.

CHAPTER TWENTY-TWO

Priyanka Varma

<u>SAND</u>

Each sand just slips down
Joining the sands of yesterday
And we cannot take them back anymore
I plea for a pause
Or a rain of sands just in our hourglass
I wish for a handful of sands as refill
Each sand just slips down
While I just stand alone, praying
To hold your hand before the falling of the last sand.

CHAPTER TWENTY-THREE

Diksha Motwani

<u>Can I?</u>
I really don't know,
What this weird feeling is for,
I just want to hug you tight,
And cry out all what's inside,
Just want to have your shoulder,
To make me relief,
I just really don't know why am feeling lone and low,
Can you please be here for me?
Can I please cry?
Can I hug you?

CHAPTER TWENTY-FOUR

Anditta Vohra

<u>Destination</u>
I look out the window
The rain is pouring heavily,
I am not able to see clearly
Whatever is infront of me.
I step out of my home
To walk in the rain,
To hide my fears
To hide my pain.
Fear of my uncertain future
Pain of being in darkness,
Afraid of what lies ahead
Everything is hazy, I dread.
Hoping that someday this rain would disappear
I'd be able to realize my worth,
The path I want to walk on
Will be closer and nearer.
The sun will shine on me brightly one day,
And guide me through my road, my way.

CHAPTER TWENTY-FIVE

Sahil Hindustani

<u>ज़िंदा</u>

ज़िंदा तो हूँ पर जान नहीं हैं

जैसे ज़मीं तो है आसमान नहीं हैं

जिसमें कभी हुआ करता था मेरा घर

आज महसूस हुआ ये वो हिंदुस्तान नहीं हैं

अल्लाह और राम में अब तुम ही करो फ़रक

एक जो बताए उनको एसा कोई ख़ानदान नहीं हैं

अब गोली मार दो चाहे गला काट दो

बचे मेरे दिल में कोई अरमान नहीं हैं

कितना बेबस हैं 'साहिल' तू इस आबो-हवा में

कि मौत का भी मिलता यहाँ सामान नहीं

Shaheen Ansari

<u>Fragrance of Love</u>
Warm, wild, chaotic aroma
Inhaled by me to the fullest
As my lungs have brimmed
With the fragrance of joy.
The smell of delicate lily
Which lits up my heart like
I want to bury it within me
And scatter it each time. I exhale.

CHAPTER TWENTY-SEVEN

Shreya Pokhriyal

<u>...The Bleeding Wound...</u>
Wounds on surface are much easy to heal,
It's not a thing which steals.
The wounds which are inside, but deep
It is very hard to define even when you take a leap.
The pain you can't share with anyone,
Even if you are with your closed one.
some words that hit hard enough, They don't need any action,
Where weapons is your reaction.
The fight without blood,
It has the same feeling when you lost someone in flood.
Everyone says time is the best medicine for healing,
But it sometimes kills your own feeling.
It's not a bleeding wound which will be fine after getting peeled off,
A truth which you have to prove it.
As only time is greatest healing medicine.

CHAPTER TWENTY-EIGHT

Jaunmarie Rheeder

<u>I see more clearly blinded...</u>

When I look at the world, I see beautiful colours.

When I close my eyes, I feel through them.

When I look at the world, I see amazing achievements.

When I close my eyes, I achieve them.

When I look at the world, I see others save places.

When I close my eyes, I have my own.

When I look at the world, I see birds flying freely.

When I close my eyes, I'm free.

When I look at the world, I see others chase their dreams.

When I close my eyes, I live in my dreams.

CHAPTER TWENTY-NINE

Sonali Ganguly

<u>एकशादीऐसीभी</u>

ना लोगों की भीड़, ना अपनों का साथ था

ना सहनाई की गूंज, ना बारात का शोर था

ना चहरे पर मुस्कान, ना बना कोई पकवान था

वो शादी थी तेरी, या दोस्तों के अरमान का ज़नाज़ा था

सगुन की थाली में मास्क, और सोशल- डिस्टिंसेंगि का दौर था

कोरोना के कहेर से मैं, कुछ इस तरह परेशान था

दोस्ती के खातिर तो, शरीख मैं भी हुआ था

सैनिटाइज़र से ना जाने, कितिनी बार नहाया था

ना शैम्पेन की बोतल, ना डिस्को का धमाका था

पैसे खूब बचाये तूने, अरमानों का गला, दोस्तों ने घोंटा था

कई खूबसूरत आँखों से टकराया मैं, फ़्लर्ट करने का भी इरादा था

बात कुछ बढ़ाने का सोचा पर, मास्क में छुपे चेहरे का क्या भरोसा था !

ना हंसी की इज़ाजत, ना बात-चीत का मौका था

तू क्या जाने पगले, दिल मेरा भी कितिना रोया था

इस दौर में शादी करने का, तुझ पर कैसा जनून सवार था

कोरोना के डर से जब, पूरा देश हुआ बर्बाद था

आबाद रहे ज़िन्दगी तेरी, मेरा ये दिल से दुआ था

ये अजब शादी की गजब कहानी, मुझे सबको सुनाना था

हाल ए दिल कुछ पंक्तियों में, बयान मुझे करना था

सतरंगी सपनो के जाल से, सबको बहार निकलना था
मस्ती में चूर, और नशे में धुत, शादी का ये पहल मुझे भी कब गवारा था
शादी मलिन है दो दिलों का, उसे भला कोरोना कहाँ रोक पाया था

CHAPTER THIRTY

Archishman Satpathy

Are you hoping for that time
    That will give you the success
    That you have had earlier as
    You fought, tried and at last won
    But what happened to that soul
    Is everything alright about that
    Or else the script plays different now
    Have you been united this time too
    Are you all making each pages
    Left turned for the next to continue
    Last time you were all together
    But are you still in that version now
    Definitely not, right? Or anything else
    Is your all hearts against your minds
    Or its the soul making the tough tour
    Be patient and knock the doors
    Of all the realistic challenges you face
    Make the most out of the lucky chances
    And once your root become stronger
    The tree of unity will surely achieve
    It will achieve the feat luck promised

Rakshith S.

It is a vast land presenting so much of joy,
    With the search of you,
    When the midst of the feel in travelling,
    For a mission in creating my vision,
    I found so lot of things which was only,
    A land filled with full of sand !
    One fine day after the reaction in an action,
    Of moments stepping ahead,
    Found an oasis just to rejuvenate with a new feel,
    To peel out in measuring the moments,
    Which is completely sparkling because of the joy filled
in us !
    (A sparkling sand is always with us in just with the
perspective of views all time beautiful)

Gauri Bangad

Leave me a text before you reach your classes...

Come back soon before it gets late..

Take a short nap before the noon ends..

Make us a call if you aren't feeling well..

Fill you stomach with more chapati's and eat the ice-cream's less...

We know you can do this let's make the way to your success then!...

The way our parents love us and care about us is just unconditional

S/O to all the lovely parents.

Let's go and give a hug to them for them being 100% supportive system for us!..

The one who has been apart from them for our studies or jobs can relate to these lines

CHAPTER THIRTY-THREE

Bishneet Kaur

<u>WHY YOU WENT AWAY?</u>
Why you gave me hope?
when you knew you were not going to come?
Why you never let me hug for the last time before just going away?
Why you didn't let me have our long deep conversations?
Why you just went away without saying a word?
Why you left me alone here in this world?
Now, who is going to protect me?
With whom am going celebrate every small moment?
I want to get angry with you but sadly you are no more with me to vanish my anger.
Now, wherever you are just see me and smile,
And feel proud as am trying to be like you,
A person with a beautiful heart and best thoughts.

CHAPTER THIRTY-FOUR

Nagaraj parshaveni

<u>Immortal magic...</u>
> my musical medicine for medicore dream,
> mesmerizing Mortifies muted my mornstream..
> misprinted moments owing to our happy dream,
> Mislayed mistakes miserable to our happy frame..
> many magical moments making me happy,
> for being without you reminds me to feel pity myself....
> Muted chat waiting for a sound and
> broken heart asking me to fill in your bond!!!

CHAPTER THIRTY-FIVE

Shalni Singh shyam

छोड ़ दिया मैंने अब उनकी परवाह करना, जिनके लिए मैं कल भी गलत थी, आज भी हूं, और शायद कल भी गलत होते रहेंगे, जिंदगी में प्यार क्या होता है।

वह उस शख्स से पूछो जिसने दिल टूटने के बाद भी इंतजार किया हो, हम सोचते थे कि मेरी यह शब्द ही चोट करते हैं, आपको हम सोचते थे कि मेरे यह शब्द ही चोट करते हैं, आपको पर कुछ खामोशियों के ज़ख्म तो और भी गहरे निकल जाते हैं।

Kasis Shaw

<u>Ironman</u>

I still remember that day,
When I was not even capable of standing on my own two feet,
At that time I had a supportive hand other than mumma's hand,
And it was definitely you.
Whenever I was threatened by a dreadful nightmare,
And found darkness too evil to deal with it alone,
I had you behind my back.
There are times in my life,
When I was getting erratic scores in the examinations,
I found you like a juxtaposed picture,
Hanging around me and instructing me not to be fragile.
I found you working days and nights,
Which is like a mystic seeking to describe the ineffable.
In all the burdensome situations,
I found you as an impenetrable barrier,
Standing and protecting me from all the fathomless obstacles,
It's true that your semblance is tough and sturdy,
But your heart is full of benevolence and love,

Your suggestions and recommendations have always helped me,
To flourish and grow.
You have given me wings to my dreams,
Which eventually made me courteous and bold,
Sometimes I found you convulsive and rebuking,
To admonish the mistakes I made,
While conquering the battle of life,
I found you so resistant,
Even in incomprehensible circumstances.
You are having a body made up of 'iron',
But a 'heart of gold',
My life would have been so unintelligible without you 'Daddy'.

CHAPTER THIRTY-SEVEN

Jayashree Sahoo

<u>Only my Father is my IDOL</u>
Always He doing well ,
For giving me best ,
He working so hard ,
For giving so happiness,
He is only one ,
Who always care me More
Who always understand me better ,
Without him ,My life is about nothing ,
He advice me for doing good work ,
Not expect for results and marks ,
He says me for focous on 100%
May be there I dont get 100
But if I ll work hard ,
Sure I get minimum 80% in my work
Only for him ,
Today I fullfilled all my dreams ..
I love you my pappa..

CHAPTER THIRTY-EIGHT

Srishti Mazumder

<u>Wander</u>
She wander around the world
in search of peace.
And returned back empty handed,
since we have forgotten that
we belong to each other.
She wander around the earth
in search of love;
and came back with a broken heart,
as there's no one with that begem.
She wander around the terra,
in search of kindness & generosity;
seeing the humanity
slaughtering & looting,
she turned back with those
dripping and swollen eyes...

CHAPTER THIRTY-NINE

Tarandeep Kaur

That time
Which was Like a sparkling sand
Has passed that I spent with you
The sand though sparkling
But never stays in hands
Even if the time is beautiful
It has to go like sand no matter what
That time
Which was like a sparkling sand
Has passed that i spent with you.
The moments spent with you
Though were very beautiful but gone
Your memories are kept even today
Even if you have gone
That time
Which was like a sparkling sand
Has passed that i spent with you.

CHAPTER FORTY

Jasmine Panda

<u>Fascinated by Nature"</u>
Being fascinated by Nature,
From the very beginning of my life,
From the changing of seasons so smoothly to the management of everything so perfectly...
From the sweet music of chirping of birds to the threatening roars in the jungles,
From the disastrous cyclones to the miraculous healing of the first rain drops,
From the dangerous volcanic eruptions to the healing sun rays in winter,
From the breathtaking dark stormy nights to the cool breezy wind,
From the beautiful colourful flowers to the tall canopy of trees,
From the vast tropical dense forest to the territorial grassy plains,
From sunrise to sunset, the whole day fascinates me,
The "NATURE", my mother, protects me, her child,
Teaches me millions of lessons of lifc....
The hills, mountains, valleys, deserts, terrains....
Fascinates me to the extreme....
Yes, fascinates me to the extreme....

Really fascinated by Nature....Mother Nature

CHAPTER FORTY-ONE

R.NATHIYA

FRIENDSHIP OF 21ˢᵗ CENTURY
FRIENDSHIP OF 21ˢᵗ CENTURY HAD
- CHANGED A LOT;
THE TIME OF VISITING IS VERY
- SHORT;
HI AND BYE IN WHATSAPP;
MEETING IN GOOGLE MEET APP;
NO VISITING OF FRIENDS HOME;
NO FEELING IN THEIR HEART BY
- OWN;
FOLLOWING FRIENDS IN SOCIAL
- MEDIA;
TO ARRANGE GET TOGETHER THERE
- IS NO IDEA;
SHARING THEIR FEELINGS AS
- MESSAGE;
TILL WE AGED;
THERE IS NO SPEAK FOR A
- LONGTIME;
THERE IS NO MEET FOR A
- LONGTIME;
THERE IS SO MANY CHANGE ;
BUT NOTHING IS STRANGE.

Shibayan Sett

<u>Home Food</u>
From having lunch in the canteen
To
Cooking for self...
We started loving
Home Food.

CHAPTER FORTY-THREE

Farida Mustafa Doctor

Last step to success
   The last step to success
   In every way is like a mess
   What's beyond is unknown
   At that point the one is alone
   All the people make a joke
   But something in the soul evoke
   Better perception , better performance
   And there on the last step is no allowance
   Of any negativity
   But only positivity.
   After that the success comes
   And famous one becomes.

CHAPTER FORTY-FOUR

Mahak Chawla

<u>BUTTERFLY</u>

Butterfly is so beautiful creature right...And yah for me and my best friend we had our pet names and so it was Butterfly and Dolphin

So here's the poem .....

I called you fly and you called me phin ,

Promised to be there in every joy and sin,

But I don't know what really happened,

You didn't cared and I got scrambled,

I wanted you to be on my side ,

Not just talk but also sit beside,

I couldn't handle the situation so well,

But thought of you to never leave me so bad,

I just cried because you were not there,

Being my bestie and not even stare,

You knew I am weak when it comes to friendship' s peak,

But still you didn't came and left me all insane ,

I missed you in every moment and so,

And I hope this happens with even you to and fro,

Not some words can express this feel,

Cause it was all above the windy breeze....

CHAPTER FORTY-FIVE

Sohini Ghosh

<u>THUNDER OF LIFE:-</u>
When I was young on rainy days,
Alone on my front porch I'd play,
I'd lose myself in another time,
That I could create with my toys and my mind.
Tomorrow never matters to me,
For that was where I would always be ,
There would be no hurt no pain no tears,
There was no worries, there was nothing to fear.
But as I grew up everything changed,
I realised that life was not a easy game.
You lived by the rules that the outside world's made,
And that feeling of safety would ultimately fade.
You walked a fine line as you faced everyday,
Filled with constant surprise as you went on your way,
And your life could change in the blink of an eye,
And failure could come no matter how hard you've tried.
You would fight many battles, as you tarried along,
Sometimes you'd be right, but most of the time you'd be wrong,
So many people you'd love and you'd hate,
But you need to keep going because life wouldn't wait.

And lost in that mess that you'd Lose everyday,
And behind all those senseless and stupid mistakes,
The moments would be so splendid, so perfect and fine,
You would wish that it could be frozen in time.
Cherished the moments with family and the fulfillment
of dreams,
Those brief special moments and the boring routines,
The excitement of learning for who you could be,
And finding that happiness wasn't guaranteed.
Discovering with relief your niche in the world,
Acheived so much but want so much more.
Through births and deaths , you'd survive just on hope.
Always searching for ways and to cope.
And then there would be love to nourish your heart,
No sadness and tears when that love fell apart.
You'd go through the stages of life as they'd come.
You'd grow up and grow old and constantly change.
You'd see beautiful things in this exceptional world,
The wonder and power of nature unfurled,
You would witness the kindness of your own human
race,
But also the destruction and chaos we make.
Indeed as a child I had no real clue,
About what was coming and what I'd go through,
And although I miss my childhood peace,
I treasure each moment that brought me to me.
But still when it dark and sad sometimes,
My cozy front porch will come gently to mine.

CHAPTER FORTY-SIX

MachJoke

<u>You're My Best Friend</u>
Mirror, You're My Best Friend,
To see my pains and sorrows,
And show me the real fact of life,
Among these dramatic humans in the world.
In anytime whenever I need some help,
The time you'll come out in front of my eyes,
Ask everything to me and conclude to solve the things,
And make my mind to goes on clear and perfectly.
Sometimes seeing my happiness in my face,
By the way you could to show me,
My chins are blowing up for my smile comes out widely,
Out of everything in my heart to fade and through away.
Mirror, The Best friend's companion that you've,
For every situation in my life and career.
Your ideas and thoughts will make surely,
Because you just lift up my mind that these are hiding
inside of myself.

CHAPTER FORTY-SEVEN

Pramila Kumari Behera

<u>Hoping</u>

In the darkest of times,
It shone so bright,
It kept us on our feet,
When life goes us so beat.
It saved us from the fall,
When the wall between us goes so tall,
It's the only thing that keeps us alive,
When we feel life's going for a dive.
It shook us from our sleep,
Sometimes it's not something we can keep,
We hold onto it for as long as we can,
But sometimes life hits up with a pan.
When we think all's lost,
When we feel like everything has gone for a toss,
It keeps the pieces of us together,
Even during the coldest of weather.
When there is nothing left us to lose and we give it our
all,
We use it to keep on going even if we have to crawl.
Remember don't give up and keep on believing,
Even when you're times of grieving,
It's the only thing that will help you in coping,

So just keep on hoping.

CHAPTER FORTY-EIGHT

HEMA KIRTHIGA J

<u>BRIGHTEST STAR!</u>
In this world full of stars!
I remain my favourite!
Because I know I am special!
Because I know how great I am!
Because I know the hardship I went through!
I have always been with me!
Through ups and down!
Throughout my life!
Hence I love myself,
A little bit more!
I am nor a narcissist!
Its just that I deserve little bit more of love!
And I am giving myself more love!
Because I love me!

CHAPTER FORTY-NINE

Dhairya Manoj Thakkar

<u>The Well Water</u>

One day, 2 farmers named Mahendra & Ashraf came to Sarpanch of their village fighting and saying that they were the victim of injustice. The Sarpanch first allowed the farmer named Mahendra to say his part. He said that he bought a well from Ashraf last week and now Ashraf is asking for money as rent of his water. Then Sarpanch allowed Ashraf to say his version. Ashraf said that he sold the well but he did not the water inside it and hence Mahendra has to pay for the water if he wanna use that water. Everyone knew that Ashraf was wrong here and he was playing with the words. Then, Sarpanch said to Ashraf, "Listen, you are right. So, do one thing. Take out all your water in one go and if there's still water left. Then, you have to pay rent of that water which is 500 Gold Coins every month to Mahendra as you're using his well for keeping your water. Ashraf was speechless and understood his mistake.

Moral :- 1.) Think out of the box. 2.) Learn to use opponent's point to target your opponent with logic.

CHAPTER FIFTY

Kareena verma

<u>The unblooming life of fates</u>

The life is full of ups & down Don't know ever where to flow & glow

Living the life , today with Hardwork Do not carry the past of handles

Do not predict about the future always

Indeed , believe in the Karma

The god of fates never be lie with times

One day Surely delightful future you have

To be your patience with Hardwork

To be light with your darkness

To be your care for your loneliness

To be your friend for your own shadow To be your tissue for your own tears Sparkling sands in your hands

Lifting alike the times no more gain The time that never be come back again

Spill your words with the bleeding ink You are the pen , you are diary of your own pain

Do not be fade away yourself in the darkness

Do not lose yourself,

Because someone is losing you ahead Wait and take a long breath with the peace

That one day when you are left this world Forever The last day of your life That everyone Remembering to you For your joy of serving,

the fates of your honest karma

CHAPTER FIFTY-ONE

Divya Vishwakarma

खुदा की एक इनायत: माँ

सबके सपने सलामत रखने के लिए, वो अपने सारे सपने दफ़नाती है,

सबकी मुस्कान बरकरार रखने के लिए, वो अपने सारे आँसू छुपाती है,

सबको पेट भर खाना खिलाने के लिए, कभी-कभी वो खुद दो निवाला कम खाती है,

सबकी खुशियों को ज़िंदा रखने के लिए, वो खुद दर्द में मरकर भी खिलखिलाती है,

सबको ज़रा सी खरोच न आ जाए, इसलिए वो हर चोट खुद सह जाती है,

सबको चैन की नींद आ जाए, इसलिए वो अपनी नींद कुरूबान कर जाती है,

सबकी सेहत ज़रा सी भी न बिगड़ जाए, इसलिए वो अपनी तबयित को नज़रंदाज़ कर देती है,

सभी रिश्ते बचाने के लिए, कभी कभी वो अपने होठं सिल लेती है,

सबको किसी भी तरह सबर न करना पड़े, इसलिए वो खुद कम में गुज़र बसर कर लेती है,

यूँ ही नहीं माँ खुदा की इनायत कहलाई जाती है।

CHAPTER FIFTY-TWO

Krishan Batra

(1) कुछ वादे जठे ही अच्छे लगते हैं,

प्यार के धागे कच्चे ही अच्छे लगते हैं,

प्यार चाहे कितना भी हो ,

लेकिन प्यार में हम बच्चे ही अच्छे लगते हैं।

(2)ज़िन्दगी दा की आ,

एह ता मिटी 'च मुक जानी आ,

प्यार गुड्डा होवे ता मौत व रुक जानी आ।

(3)मौसम बदलिआ,दुनयिा बदली,

पर तेरी दती होई तन्हाई ना बदली,

खूबसूरत इनी के मोतियां नाल सजा दयै,

इना व ना खोइए के आप नू ही भुला दयैो

(4)काश सं भाल पाती ये रात उस बात को,

दलि में छुपा पाती उस जस्बात को,

काश भुला पाती उस मुलाकात को,

या वक्त पर जता पाती उस एहसास को ।

(5)ये रात तो ढल जाएगी,

खुद को कैसे समझाओगे

अगले दनि फरि आयेगी,

इससे बात कैसे छुपाओगे।

CHAPTER FIFTY-THREE

Soumili Sarkar

<u>Lacking of listeners,</u>
Many were only spectators!
Never thought that pens are sharper than swords!
Loneliness covered,
Searching those who stayed unremembered.
Cheerful, enthusiastic, talkative girl was quite.
Noone bothered to look at my sight.
A 16years old girl wanna ride high.
There was noone who was only my!
Stopped thinking about them for a while.
Closed my eyes moved to toil.
Discovered a new me,
Who was quite but not words free!
Grabbed the pen,
Hold tight and jumped in the writing lane!♡

CHAPTER FIFTY-FOUR

K Meghasyam

"LIVE FOR A CAUSE " Life the beautiful word. It gives us with many things. It's an un explainable and the confusing ever topic we can discuss up on. The discussion if started would not have an end. It can be experessed in number if novels or books we wish to. It provides us with wide opportunities. But we fail ti recognise it. Everyone in this world believe in god. Even the atheist at some point of time would be a believer in the almighty. The almighty is present in everyone of us. There is some supreme power surely present. The acts which are started with selfless aim are surely successful. The success is assured. Instead of just being self oriented and working on own development. Work for giving something back to the society and people where you got an opportunity to live. There comes my tile to LIVE FOR A CAUSE. only then the wonderful word LIFE will have some meaning added to it. Think over it my friends. Let the LIFE we lived be am example for our future generations. This leads for a man to live in the hearts of people even after we leave this world. We are gonna be alive im the hearts of people.

DIGAMARTHI ATCHYUTH

<u>NATURE</u>

Nature is a beautiful entity on this planet. It's has a way of life, packed with virtues. It doesn't talk, but is successful in letting the human beings transpire many wonders. It can symbolize peace(serene forests) , ire(natural disasters), sorrow(dried plants), joy(blossoms) and so on. We can infer from this that the perfect blend of every piece of creation on this Earth lets the birthing of a tranquil stint.

Humans shall explore nature, not exploit. A big tree gives shade to small plants and creatures, this signifies the quality

of being humble enough to be a generous benefactor. Symbiosis, a phenomenon in which plants mutually benefit to support each other's survival, this tells us the importance of inter dependence. A parasite mimics the role of such evils who encash on somebody's efforts. But had there been no parasites(challenges) we wouldn't have strived to become strong.

It's the best physician. It does not see a doctor for illness. It knows that it can recover itself with the passage

of time,that's self reliance. Trees can grow inordinately, but they originate from a tiny seed. So size isn't what matters it's the quality that defines our worth. Even the death of the plants isn't going in vain, it becomes manure and turns out to be useful for another plant.
So lets be optimistic and inquisitive to stand some purpose for being fortunate to live and prosper with fortitude.

Twisha Ray

These are the hands
That hold a pen
That help me to write
Now, and again
These are the hands
That i can count my fingers
To work out a sum
When my mind lingers
These are the hands
When joined with another
That expresses fondness
And desire for a lover
These are the hands
That i stuck in the air
When knowing the answer
To a question, so there!
These are the hands
That held my thumb on my nose
Then wriggled my fingers
For a cheeky pose!
These are the hands
That played with toys
And clapped together

To make some noise
These are the hands
That ive had all my life
That despite their beginning
I am now their wife...
These are the hands
With sensually creative fingers
That caressed my lovers
For an orgasm that lingers
These are the hands
That will forever offer peace
And will occasionally help me
Eat chocolate, or cheese!

CHAPTER FIFTY-SEVEN

Soniya Varghese

<u>Conquered Thoughts</u>
The way you couldn't sleep at nights,
The way you struggled to get a sleep.
A lighted cigarette and a book to write in.
Stars and moon accompanying you,
All the lonesome feelings alongside.
Now you can't control your sleep,
Asking me what have I done to you.
Maybe because you've lost your lonesome feelings,
Or maybe because you've finally found your peace.
It can be anything or is it me?
Whatever it maybe, but I like,
The way you sleep while talking to me.
And the way you apologize for sleeping.
You're the sweetest macho man I've ever met.
You had those sleepless nights where ,
Thoughts conquered you on a piece of paper.
Now you're the one who's conquering the thoughts,
Which a mere piece of paper can't hold with it.

CHAPTER FIFTY-EIGHT

B Pavan Kumar

<u>"My unsaid feelings to her"</u>

"It isn't the good bye that hurts you, but the flashback that follows"

I want to stare at those annoying eyes which had great feelings for me

I want you to slap me for the breakup I asked for

I want to have those late night conversations, that separated us

I thought you might be the worst chapter of my book but later.... I realized you are my complete book!!

We are who we choose to be not the one who we pretend to be

I want to kiss your hand where you had the deepest cut for me

I want you to remain the same whom I loved unconditionally,

I want to ask you,

If nothing lasts forever, would you allow me to be your nothing..

CHAPTER FIFTY-NINE

MD KALIMUDDIN

"हिन्दोस्तांकीआजादलफ्ज"
लो कफन बाँधे वो चला,
अपने भारत माँ की आबरू बचानो
दुश्मनों को धूल चटानो
और काफिरों को नरक पहुंचानो
अजीब सी इश्क़ हैं इस मिट्टी से,
जहाँ राम और रहीम साथ रहते हौं
उसी गंगा में पूजा करते हौं
उसी गंगा में वज़ू भी करते हौं
अगर कुछ ना कर सके इसके लिए,
तो इस रग में बहती खून का क्या?
उस भाईचारे और बलदिान का क्या?
तिरंगा से लिपटे उनकी शहादत का क्या?
यूं पल भर में ना महान बना देश,
प्रत्येक जनगण की भागीदारी रही।
हिंसा पर अहिंसा हमेशा भारी रही।
और नफ़रतों पर मोहब्बत भारी रही।

CHAPTER SIXTY

Tripti Pradhan

<u>NUDITY</u>

Every one is keen about what's under the clothes
Every one wants to go inside your clothes
But now one is keen to know about whats under the skin.
No one want to know what's inside
Going under the skin , seeing the soul is the true nudity

.

Nudity is exposure of your oneselves but how can you being in the body without being to the soul of the body its just like visiting the temple without confronting god no sense haa!!! Exactly say as our body how can you know just being with physicality what's about the actuality .

Bodies can be build up but soul can't body can be healed but soul can't. Non other than exposing someone's body , be more generous to expose someone's soul.

Let your hand touch the soul
Open the curtain of your being
Clothe yourselves in nudity
Uncover the souls of the body
Invent a new soul for your body...

Bharti Sahu

अगर डरते हो हारने से,
    तो हौसला रखना सीखो,
    अगर जीतने की ख़्वाहिश है,
    तो आगे बढ़ना सीखो।

Shreshth Lata Sahu

<u>The Moon Light</u>
The moon light is the shower of peace
It makes your soul calm,
but the moon is not the owner of it
At night it comes
make the time slow
and let the people know that it has something to glow
let it moisturize the hard corners of your heart
let it give you some feeling so you can
liv the rest part
It can remove the darkness of your soul
let it come to your home
It will suppress the sorrowness
and give your the clear path
Don't be so thankful of moon ,now
Cause,
Once it became jealous because it has no light
But then,
Sun stands and let moon become bright
from then it happening every night

CHAPTER SIXTY-THREE

Nikita kumari

दयालु

इस युग में तो सब मतलबी मिलते,
जो अपना भला ही सोचते,
दूसरो से इनको मतलब नहीं,
उनके दर्द से इनको सहानुभूति नहीं।
देख कर मुंह फेर लेते,
तो कभी इनके पुकारो को ठुकराते,
जैसे इन्होने देखा ही नहीं,
इन में तो या ही नहीं।
उन में से कुछ लोग ऐसे होते,
जो आगे आते,
उनके दर्द को समझते,
और यथासंभव सहयोग करतो
जनि में थोडा भी स्वार्थ नहीं,
करते किसी का अहति नहीं,
वही तो है दयालु,
जो है दिल से कृपालु।

CHAPTER SIXTY-FOUR

Ankita Nahar

सुनो ना
सब कहते हैं मुझे
मोहब्बत है तुमसे
शायद सही कहते हो
हां माना मोहबब्त है तुमसे
पर खुद से उससे भी ज्यादा है
ये कहा नहीं कभी मैंने तुमसे
हां माना अच्छे लगते हो तुम हमें
पर खुद से ज्यादा नहीं लगते
ये कहा नहीं कभी मैंने तुमसे
हां माना परवाह है तुम्हारी
पर खुद की उससे भी ज्यादा है
ये कहा नहीं कभी मैंने तुमसे
पर आज इतना सा कहूंगी मैं तुमसे
मोहबब्त है तुमसे
पर खुद से
बेइंतहा मोहब्बत है

Mahi Adlakha

It takes every ounce of me,
To see what others see,
Stories end on their time,
Don't you think it's time for mine?
Fairies and bunny ears,
Even clouds shed their tears,
Maybe we don't part ways,
Maybe we just count the day,
How miserable our lives we made,
But I'll hurt more now,
As free trials over,
Now it's paid.

Thank You!

This book is heart and soul of these authors they have pored thier heart out. Give them love and suppport , thank you and spread the sparkle.

Our Co Authors

Complier Srizen Khaneja

Enter Caption